Michael M. Dediu

If You Want Peace, Prepare for Peace!

Moving from preparing for war, to preparing for peace

DERC Publishing House
Tewksbury (Boston), Massachusetts, U. S. A.

Published and printed in the
United States of America
On the Great Seal of the United States are included:
E Pluribus Unum (Out of many, one)
Annuit Coeptis (He has approved of the undertakings)
Novus Ordo Seclorum (New order of the ages)

Library of Congress Control Number: 2019919132

Dediu, Michael M.

If You Want Peace, Prepare for Peace!
Moving from preparing for war, to preparing for peace

ISBN-13: 978-1-950999-04-0

MSG0232605_04at3RbGK96w49ma0OWD
MSG0233385_Zbe8Ji0KaxTED6yCVmK9
1-8292825611
1-3T5C1A7
07456D
26LOOF7G
1-3T5C1AE

Preface

Just about 1625 years ago, during the Roman Emperor Flavius Theodosius Augustus, or Theodosius the Great, the Roman general Publius Flavius Vegetius Renatus, around 394, wrote in Latin the book "Epitoma Rei Militaris" or "De re militari" (Concerning Military Matters), in which he mentions "Igitur qui desiderat pacem, praeparet bellum", later simplified as "Si vis pacem, para bellum", which means "If you want peace, prepare for war".

Well, after over 1625 years of wars after wars after wars, the over 7.7 billions of people on Earth demand a change:
Si vis pacem, para PACEM!

No need to translate, but if you insist:
If you want peace, prepare for PEACE!

On 24 November 2019 Pope Francis called for a 'world without nuclear weapons' during his Nagasaki visit.

Using a lovely imaginary dialog between Sun and Earth, this book is exactly what we need to really prepare for peace, with clear and practical ideas, which will help the over 7.7 B people to have a **Harmonious World, with Sustainable Peace, Freedom, Health, Friendship and Prosperity.**

Michael M. Dediu, Ph. D.

Tewksbury (Boston), U. S. A., 25 November 2019

USA, New York: On Fifth Avenue at E 40th St, looking southwest at Mid-Manhattan Library, a New York Public Library (1895, 1908, 87 branches (Carnegie libraries (Andrew Carnegie (1835-1919))), 53 millions of books and other items, the 2nd largest public library in the United States (behind the Library of Congress), and the fourth largest in the world (after British Library (170 M), Library of Congress (160 M), and Library and Archives Canada (54 M)) image archive (left), having thousands of photos, posters, illustrations, and other images.

Table of Contents

1 – World is a family of 7.7 billions of people

SUN: My dear Earth, let's start with this good news: on 24 November 2019, Pope Francis called for a 'world without nuclear weapons' during his Nagasaki visit.

How are you?

USA, Washington: Woodrow Wilson International Center for Scholars (1968). There is now the 1913 Centennial, in celebration of the 100th anniversary of President Woodrow Wilson's inauguration.

EARTH: Your Highness SUN, pretty good so far, and I am very happy to hear the good news, thank you, but our situation could be much better. Let's now remember a few details about the Roman Emperor Flavius Theodosius Augustus, or Theodosius the Great (11 January 347, Italica (now in Spain) – 17 January 395, Mediolanum (now Milano, Italy), aged 48 years and 6 days; emperor for 13.3

years in the East: 9 January 379 (age 31.9) – 15 May 392 (age 45.3), then emperor over the whole empire for 2.7 years, total 16 years and 8 days: 15 May 392 – 17 January 395).

And you?

SUN: Well, working hard to keep all the planets happy, you see…For simplicity, call me Sun.

Yes, you are right, it could be much better.

Do you remember that joke about you?

EARTH: What joke?!

SUN: Your friend Mars asked you, how are you?

EARTH: And what I said.

SUN: You said that you got a cold or something, and have a lot of people on you….

EARTH: And what Mars responded?

SUN: Mars was very kind: don't warry Earth, Mars said, it will pass……………

EARTH: Good joke, but, you see, if my people – who are all scared stiff of this continuation of preparation for war – don't change quickly to preparing for peace, then one day they will really pass…

SUN: Exactly - for this we need to discuss how to change from preparing to war, to preparing for peace.

EARTH: I agree 100%. The family of over 7.7 billions of people wants peace.

SUN: Of course, and when they will have a friendly, helpful, fast, polite, modest and very smart world management, it will be easy to maintain peace.

EARTH: But until then what do we do? Because right now the situation is really bad: the world is facing serious threats and challenges. There are many uncertainty factors. The military technology is developing rapidly, while competition and rivalry are growing stronger and morphing into new forms. There are old smoldering conflicts in various regions of the planet, and new ones keep appearing. The leading countries are actively developing their offensive weapons. The nuclear club is receiving new members. The NATO infrastructure is expanding. There are efforts to militarize outer space. There is broad use of artificial intelligence in creating military arms, in particular reconnaissance and attack unmanned aerial vehicles, laser and hypersonic systems, and weapons based on new principles of physics, as well as robotic systems capable of performing a variety of tasks on the battlefield.

They prepare for war day and night!

USA, New York: W 42nd Street, near 8th Avenue, with the Chrysler Building (1930, 320 m, 77 floors, center-right far back).

Italy, Roma: Piazza del Campidoglio has three main Palazzi. Palazzo Senatorio (back, now Rome's city hall), built around 1250-1350 atop the Tabularium (78 BC, housed the archives of the ancient Rome), re-used blocks from the Tabularium, and was modified by Michelangelo around 1535. The Palazzo dei Conservatori (right) was built around 1550, for the local magistrate, on top of a temple (about 550 BC) dedicated to Jupiter "Maximus Capitolinus". Michelangelo's renovation of it incorporated many new architectural ideas. Palazzo Nuovo (left) was built around 1650, based on Michelangelo's ideas, with an identical exterior design to the Palazzo dei Conservatori, which it faces across the piazza. The Capitoline Museums are inside all these three Palazzi surrounding the Piazza del Campidoglio, and interlinked by an underground gallery beneath the piazza. Until around 1475, the main market of the city of Rome was held on and around the Piazza del Campidoglio, while cattle continued to be taxed and sold in the ancient forum located just to the south. Michelangelo Buonarroti (1475 – 1564) had a key role in the design and updating of the Piazza del Campidoglio and its surrounding Palazzi.

Start discussions

SUN: Start talking at different levels.

EARTH: What would it be the best level to start with?

SUN: Military – they will be the first to suffer if something bad happens, therefore they should begin to discuss to change the current enemies into friends.

EARTH: Indeed, instead of building very dangerous arms to destroy each other, and millions of people around them, better start building beautiful houses for them, for their families, their friends, and for others, with the budgets they already have.

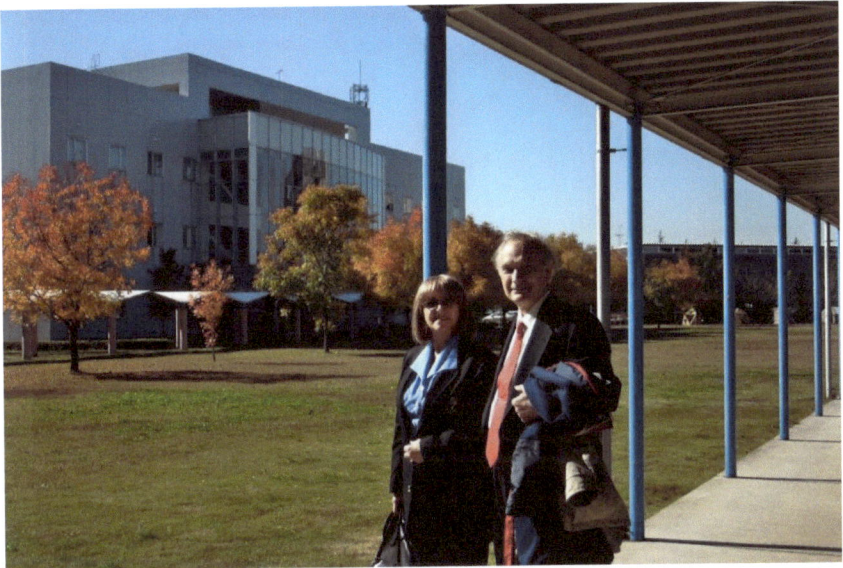

Japan: Another building (left), seen from a small laboratory, on the south part of the Inzai (Chiba) campus of Tokyo Denki University (TDU, founded in 1907), in Muzai-Gakuendai, 34 km north-east of Tokyo.

Change school history books

SUN: Instead of telling kids all the terrible wars each country had all the time, tell them of the beautiful peace which existed between the wars, in which time, by the way, all the important things on Earth happened.

EARTH: Yes, this is long overdue.

Finland, Helsinki: a commercial harbor in the south-west of the city, near Hietalahdenranta, with the boat Aranda.

Begin to visit each other more frequently

SUN: Are your people visiting each other frequently?

EARTH: Not much. Visiting people in others countries should be much more intense.

SUN: And make friends everywhere.

EARTH: Exactly! I'd love to see them all being friends!

Italy, Roma: Detail from the left side of the fountain in front of the staircase of Palazzo Senatorio, showing the river god of the Tiber.

2- Levels of World Peaceful Collaboration

SUN: In order to make you happy, there should be several levels of establishing peaceful cooperation:
- family
- school
- university
- company
- city
- counties
- provinces or regions (states in the U.S)
- country
- United Nations

EARTH: This is what we need – let's go to more details.

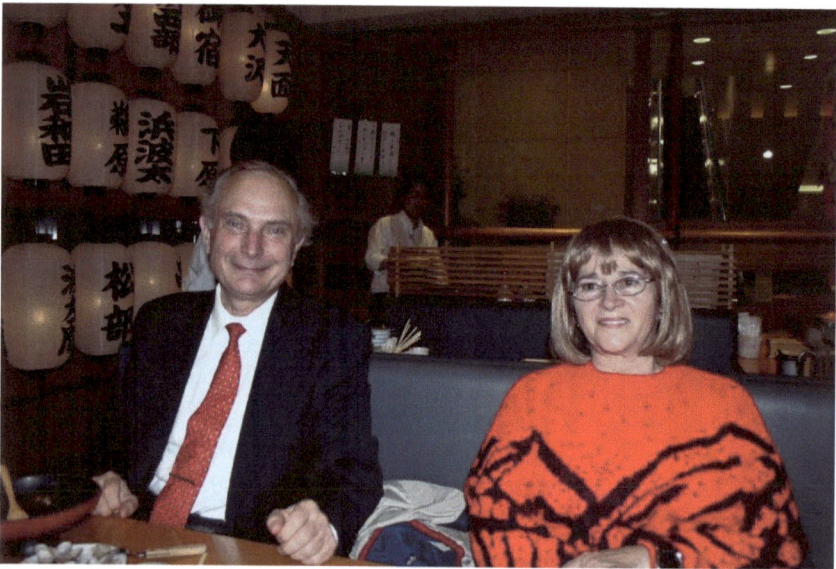

Japan: At a revolving sushi bar in Tokyo, with the conveyor belt on the right, and rotating cylinders with light inside for the seven Gods of Fortune: Benzaiten, Daikokuten, Ebisu, Hotei, Jurōjin, Fukurokuju and Bishamonten (left).

Family Peaceful Collaboration

SUN: How many families do you have?

EARTH: I have around 3 billions of families (I included also the singles as a temporary family of one person).

SUN: Great! Each family should be in peaceful collaboration with at least 3 other families from 3 different countries.

EARTH: Wonderful! They should maintain contact by e-mails, phone, mails and visits. The family is the foundation of the society on Earth. It is at home, in the lap of the family, that we receive the basics of our worldview, develop our personal qualities, and absorb practical, cultural and spiritual ideals. It is very important to bring up the younger generation in the spirit and on the values of a large and close-knit family with many children, where everyone, both children and parents, takes care of each other, and to create conditions for the professional and creative fulfilment of young people, as well as the settlement of essential social and practical problems. The healthcare system must be reliable, and strong support should be given to the pro-natal population policy, young families, mothers, fathers and children.

France, Paris (founded circa 250 BC): The Arc de Triomphe de l'Étoile (honors those who died for France after 1792), 1836, height 50 m, wide 45 m, deep 22 m, in the center of the Place Charles de Gaulle (Place de l'Étoile), at the western end of the Champs-Élysées.

School Peaceful Collaboration

SUN: How many K-12 students do you have?

EARTH: I have around 1.3 billion enrolled students in primary and secondary schools, but there are many children between 7 and 18 who are not enrolled in schools yet.

SUN: This is a major issue which must be addressed. And how many schools do you have?

EARTH: I have around 3 millions of schools.

SUN: Then each school should be in contact with at least 4 other school from different countries, for peaceful collaboration.

EARTH: Children could learn from graphical coding for pre-readers to full-text coding for high schoolers, if they stick to science and technology.

SUN: Yes – and this could inspire them to become builders, mathematicians, musicians, engineers, artists, physicists, doctors, etc.

Allocate war-related money to having all school-age kids in schools

EARTH: Yes, we really need to allocate war-related money to having all school-age kids in schools – it's just a matter of common sense!

SUN: Of course, and it is much cheaper than building some huge destructive arms.

EARTH: Cheaper and much better for the future.

Italy, Roma: Detail from the right side of the fountain in front of the staircase of Palazzo Senatorio, showing the river god of the Nile.

University Peaceful Collaboration

SUN: Some universities have already good collaboration with others, but this should be extended and improved – each university to have peaceful collaboration with at least 5 universities from different countries and continents.

EARTH: Yes, they can really establish some high standards of peaceful collaboration, which should be an example for all.

Japan: Photographs and a layout of the High Energy Accelerator (center-left), at the High Energy Accelerator Research Organization (KEK, 1997) in Tsukuba Science City (1962), in Ibaraki Prefecture, 60 km north-east of Tokyo.

Company Peaceful Collaboration

SUN: Companies, and any other type of institutions and organizations, should have extensive peaceful collaboration with others from other countries – it is good for business and for peace.

EARTH: And for beginning to substitute the production of war devices with peaceful devices, useful for everybody. Some small companies, which are interested in this, are speaking up now, because they are uniquely worried that the current unstable situation will dry up the venture capital funding that drives their industry and, in turn, make it impossible for the small startups, that turn basic research into new products or medicines, to get off the ground.

USA, Boston: a tall ship (center-left), Spirit of Boston boat (right).

City Level Peaceful Collaboration

SUN: Many cities are already in contact between them, but this should be generalized: each city should have peaceful collaboration with at least 7 other cities from different countries and continents.

EARTH: Yes, we badly need this. For example, Venice: Venetians woke Wednesday. 13 Nov, to distressing scenes after the highest tide in 50 years washed through the historic Italian city, beaching gondolas, trashing hotels, and sending tourists fleeing through rapidly rising waters. It was an exceptional overnight "Alta Acqua" high tide water level. The extraordinarily intense "acqua alta," or high waters, peaked at 1.87 m. Only once, since records began in 1923, has the water crept even higher, reaching 1.94 m in 1966.

They need a lot of help.

USA, Boston (founded in 1630): tall ships from many countries, at the Boston Fish Pier (opened in 1915).

County Level Peaceful Collaboration

SUN: Counties are not yet too interested, but you never know.

EARTH: Actually, some like the idea, and there is hope that each county will have peaceful collaboration with at least 8 counties from the world.

Italy, Roma: Forum Romanum (80 BC, right), Temple of Saturn 42 BC, center, Arch of Severus 203, center-left, Temple of Vespasian 80, left.

Province Level Peaceful Collaboration

SUN: This is an important level, and their commitment to a peaceful collaboration with at least 9 provinces (or states in the U.S.) from different countries and continents would be a great contribution to peace.

EARTH: I cannot wait for this.

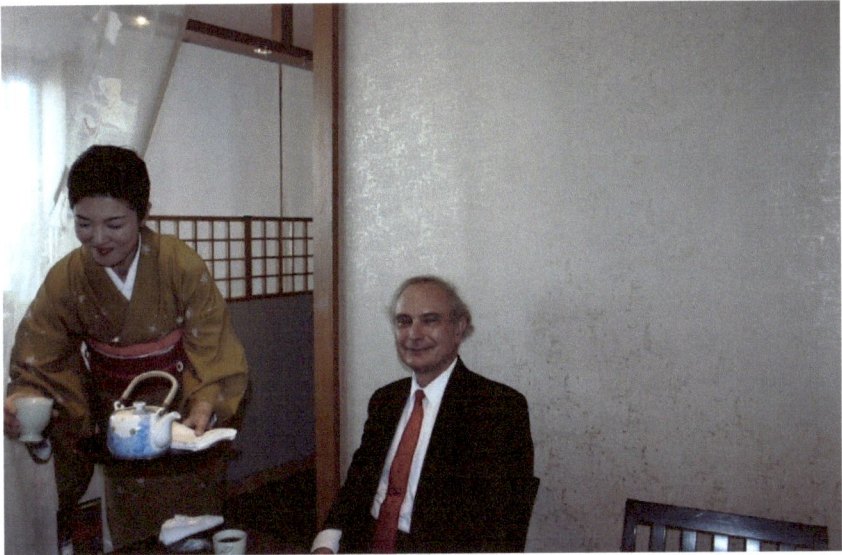

Japan: In a delightful classical Japanese restaurant, with exquisite Japanese food and service, in Tsukuba Science City (founded in 1962), in Ibaraki Prefecture, 60 km north-east of Tokyo.

Country Level Peaceful Collaboration

SUN: Now we arrived at the most significant level, were, actually, the whole issue can be totally solved.

EARTH: Yes, indeed. There is now only one war related treaty, created 70 years ago against Stalin, who died less than 4 years later, then 36 years later his country USSR disappeared, two years after that the other opposite war related Warsaw treaty also disappeared, after 36 years of existence, but this 70 years old superfluous war treaty increased to 29 countries, and still takes people's money for war.

SUN: You remember what Reagan said, do you?

EARTH: Sure, he even mentions me: "No government ever voluntarily reduces itself in size. Government programs, once launched, never disappear. Actually, a government bureau is the nearest thing to eternal life we'll ever see on this earth!"

SUN: If this eternal war treaty, which became a bastion of bad ideas, would be changed into a peace treaty, and invite all the other countries on Earth to join it, you have peace on Earth!

EARTH: I don't need anything else!

USA, New York: West 42nd Street near 7th Avenue and Times Square, with many tall buildings around, like the Conde Nast Building (1996-1999, 264 m, 48-story office tower, on the left).

United Nations Level Peaceful Collaboration

SUN: Finally, United Nations, certainly, do many useful peace-related tasks, however something is missing.

EARTH: Yes, they need to work at the people level, not only at the government level.

SUN: Indeed, they should contact all the people in the world, and promote peaceful collaboration.

EARTH: Peace must be built from ground up.

Finland, Helsinki: a Baltic Sea canal from west to east, near Ruoholahdenpuisto, seen from a bridge on Bottenhavsgatan, near Helsinki Conservatory of Music (left).

3 – Peaceful Collaboration Management

SUN: All this peaceful collaboration at different levels needs some small management.

EARTH: Yes, at each level they should elect a manager to coordinate the work, to keep the financial records and other records. All the money will be deposited in a bank account.

SUN: It is clear that this peaceful collaboration will bring good practical results.

EARTH: And it will create a peaceful atmosphere, which will reduce the risk of war.

SUN: Also, it will create favorable conditions to implement what our friend Michael M. Dediu described in his books "Our Future is Sustainable Peace and Prosperity – Moving from conflicts to harmony and peace", "Our Future Depends on Good World Educations – Moving from frail education to solid education", and "Friendly, Helpful & Smart World Management - Moving from bureaucracy to responsive world management".

EARTH: All over 7.7 B people want this.

UK, London: From the Bow Street, the northeast façade of the Royal Opera House at Covent Garden (1732, 1808, 1858, 1999, capacity 2,256). In 1734, Covent Garden presented its first ballet, Pygmalion. On 14 January 1947, the Covent Garden Opera Company gave its first performance of Carmen (1875, opera in four acts, based on a novella of the same title by Prosper Mérimée (1803-1870 (age 67))) by French composer Georges Bizet (1838-1875 (age 36)).

Small Budget

SUN: As this collaboration and preparing for peace advances, some small budgets at different levels will be necessary.

EARTH: Yes, and these small budgets for peace preparation can very easily be taken from the huge war budgets of the world – total over $1.6 T in 2015, around $215/person. The U.S. accounted for 37% of the total, in 2018 it was $639 B, or $1955/person. Just 1% of this war budget would mean $16 B for peace.

SUN: A lot of money wasted on war related things. How many average houses for families could have been built in 2015 with this wasted money?

EARTH: Over 10 M houses for over 30 M people.

Italy, Roma: The fountain in front of the staircase of Palazzo Senatorio features the river gods of the Nile (left) and Tiber (right), and Dea Roma (Minerva, center).

No abuses

SUN: It is expected to have strict discipline and no abuses in this preparation for peace.

EARTH: Yes, the managers and all the people should pay attention to this.

Japan: Photographs with celebrity physicists and chemists, like Ernest Rutherford (1871 - 1937, who is considered the father of nuclear physics, center-right down), at the High Energy Accelerator Research Organization (KEK, 1997) in Tsukuba Science City (1962), in Ibaraki Prefecture, 60 km north-east of Tokyo,

Volunteers

SUN: Volunteers will be needed.

EARTH: They are always welcome to join the growing group of people preparing for peace.

Finland, Helsinki Central railway station (1907 – 1914), on Brunnsgatan, in the city center.

Permanent contact with all people

SUN: An important aspect of this preparation for peace is the permanent contact with all people.

EARTH: Yes, by visiting them, phone calls, e-mails, videos, and mail, to keep everybody calm, friendly and peace oriented.

SUN: Then the transfer to a sustainable peace, freedom and prosperity will be easy.

EARTH: All the people want exactly this.

Italy, Roma: The Arch of Septimius Severus (145 – 211, Emperor 193 - 211), built in 203.

Common language and alphabet

SUN: When preparing for peace, it will be normal to have a common language and alphabet on Earth.

EARTH: Certainly, and because English is a de facto common language now, it will be taken as the basis of the world language, let's call it Mundo, which will be taught in all schools and used in the world government.

SUN: All the other languages will continue as secondary languages.

EARTH: Yes, and the same is true for the Latin alphabet, which will be used everywhere, with other alphabets as secondary.

Japan: A slice from 840 years old cryptomeria japonica conifer, from 1950, with white marks for every 100 years, in Tsukuba Science City (1962), in Ibaraki Prefecture, 60 km north-east of Tokyo.

Work for everybody

SUN: The beauty is that this preparation for peace gives work to everybody.

EARTH: Indeed, if unemployed, this is a temporary job, at world minimum wage ($2/hour), until they find a better job.

SUN: But also, for those who don't look for a job – this is a nice and very useful hobby.

EARTH: And you will be in contact with many interesting and friendly people.

USA: Washington, D.C. (founded 1790) United States Capitol (1793 – 1800, 88 m), seen from the west, near the Reflecting Pool.

Donations

SUN: Those interested in making donations, this preparing for peace is a good cause.

EARTH: Taking into account that the 2018 Global Wealth Report from Credit Suisse shows that total global wealth has now reached $317 trillions (circa $41,000/person), just a tiny 0.01% donation would mean $31.7 B.

SUN: This would visibly advance the preparation for peace.

EARTH: And this peace would obviously bring a tri-fold increase in Global Wealth!

Italy, Roma: Temple of Saturn 42 BC, right, Arch of Severus 203, center-right, Temple of Vespasian 80 center, east side of Palazzo Senatorio, left.

UK, Oxford: From Broad St, looking south to the northeastern side of the Sheldonian Theatre (1669, classical concerts, lectures, capacity 1,000, by Gilbert Sheldon (1598-1677, Archbishop of Canterbury), 3 busts (center line), Bodleian Library (1602, left back, main research library of the University of Oxford, over 12 M items).

Tax Department

SUN: At the tax level, it would be very appropriate to have on the last line of the tax form, just before the signature, a very simple question: How much of this tax do you want to go for peaceful purposes?

EARTH: Oh, yes! This would be a very direct reply from the people on how much they really want to spend on peace-related things, as oppose to war-related.

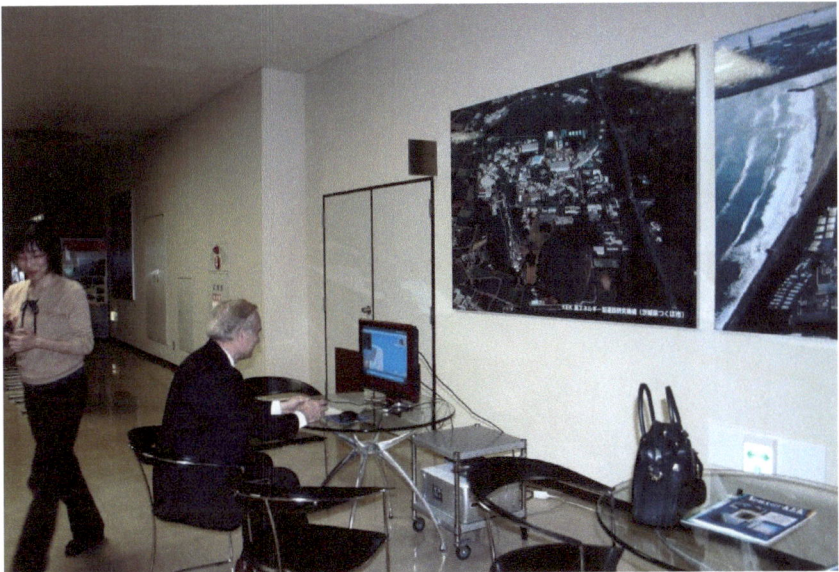

Japan: Photographs and computer presentations at the High Energy Accelerator Research Organization (KEK, 1997) in Tsukuba Science City (1962), in Ibaraki, 60 km north-east of Tokyo.

Current government buildings and equipment

SUN: Also, some of the current government buildings and equipment should be used for preparation for peace.

EARTH: Yes, not all government buildings and equipment are used 100%, therefore there is room for some people preparing for peace.

Finland, Helsinki: The Railway Square, east of the railway station, the bus station (left) and the Finnish National Theatre (center-left).

4 - Preparation for Peace Institut

SUN: If enough money and people are available, a Preparation for Peace Institut (PPI) should be created.

EARTH: Yes, a non-profit organization dedicated to preparation for peace.

Italy, Roma: On Ponte Palatino (1891), Pons Cestius (46 BC, left), Isola Tiberina (center), Basilica San Bartolomeo all'Isola (990, center).

Assisting people on peaceful objectives

SUN: This PPI will help people on all peace-related tasks.

EARTH: Including savings accounts, mortgages, small business advice, no homelessness, etc.

Japan: Mount Fuji (3,776 m, 1707 last eruption) seen from Kawaguchi city (left), near Kawaguchiko (Lake Kawaguchi, 6 km^2, 830 m elevation, right), 100 km south-west of Tokyo.

No bureaucracy

SUN: Certainly, PPI will help to eliminate bureaucracy as much as possible.

EARTH: Firstly, they will set an example themselves, and then help others.

USA, Washington (1790), National Gallery of Art (1937, National Mall)

Receiving comments from people

SUN: PPI will invite comments from people on preparing for peace issues.

EARTH: Always there are people with good ideas, and some even with resources to work for peace.

Italy, Roma: La Bocca della Verità (50 AD) is a sculpture carved from Pavonazzo marble, with a man-like face (Oceanus).

No violence

SUN: Eliminating corruption, organized crime and drug trafficking is helpful for peace.

EARTH: Yes, violent activities must be eliminated in order to have peace. For example, since 2006, over 150,000 Mexicans have been murdered in drug wars. Also, in 2018 there were 16 journalists killed, and 37 local officials and candidates killed. A drug cartel earns more than $3 B/year. This situation must be completely changed by severe police intervention.

USA, Washington (1790), National Archives and Records Administration building (1935), on Constitution Avenue.

Japan: Shinjuku is a ward of Tokyo, with many very tall buildings.

Peace volunteers

SUN: Naturally PPI will focus on peace volunteers.

EARTH: They will play a key role in this worldwide preparation for peace.

USA, Finland, Helsinki: in the south of the Railway Square is the Ateneum (1887, a major museum of classical art).

Harmony

SUN: Helping people to be friendly and happy, to live in harmony, is exactly what PPI wants.

EARTH: And this is the shortest way to achieve a peaceful world.

Italy, Roma: The Basilica Santa Maria in Cosmedin (1085) with the Bocca della Verità (Mouth of Truth) in its porch

Family assistance

SUN: Everything starts with the family, therefore PPI will always assist families.

EARTH: Everybody in the world has a mother and a father, and peace is very important for all of them.

USA, Washington (1790), Smithsonian National Museum of Natural History (1910, with wings added in the 1960s, with 126 millions of objects), on the National Mall, on Constitution Avenue NW.

Dispute resolution

SUN: Peace without dispute resolution is not possible.

EARTH: PPI will have a big role in helping with dispute resolution everywhere.

France, Paris: La Tour Eiffel (1889, 324 m, 279 m third level observatory) seen from 2 km north at l'Arc de Triomphe de l'Étoile (1836, 50 m).

Informing people

SUN: It goes without saying that PPI must continuously inform people on its activities and results.

EARTH: It must be short and clear – people don't have time to read or listen to long and confusing stories.

Italy, Roma: The Circus Maximus (550 BC – 549 AD), the world largest stadium (250,000 people) for chariot races, for over 1,000 years.

Election assistance

SUN: Elections are important, and PPI will carefully support candidates who have a good record of supporting peace, freedom, health and prosperity.

EARTH: Also, PPI will support civilized, polite and courteous elections.

UK, Oxford: On High St. at Merton St, looking northwest to University Church of St Mary the Virgin (1252, a church adopted as the first building of Oxford University (1096, Dominus Illuminatio Mea (The Lord is my Light)).

Tokyo Metropolitan Government Building, 243 m, 48 floors, 1991, in Shinjuku, with two observation decks on floor 45, 202 m.

Membership cards

SUN: PPI will issue membership cards to its members.

EARTH: These cards will be useful for accessing buildings and events organized by PPI.

USA, New York (1624): on 7th Avenue in Times Square, with the Bertelsmann Building (1990, 223 m, 44 floors, center-right).

No abuses

SUN: When abuses happen, PPI will calmly assist people to correct the situation.

EARTH: When somebody from government is abusive, special efforts from PPI will be needed.

Italy, Roma: Part of the Imperial Palaces (27 BC) on the Palatine Hill.

Mediation

SUN: Everything under the Sun needs mediation from time to time.

EARTH: And PPI definitively will help, mediation and conciliation being closely related to peace.

Finland, Helsinki: The Three smiths statue (by Felix Nylund, 1932), with the Old Student House (1870) in the back, near the crossing of Aleksanterinkatu (right) and Mannerheimintie (left).

UK, Oxford: From the Logic Ln, looking north to the High St and the south gate of the Queen's College (1341, founded by Robert de Eglesfield (1295-1349, chaplain of the Queen consort) in honor of Queen consort Philippa of Hainault (1314-1369, wife of Edward III of England (1312-1377, Reign 1327-1377, burial Westminster Abbey, they had 13 children, and their great-grandfather was King Philip III of France (1245-1285, reign 1270-1285))), University College (1249, left).

People movement assistance

SUN: When people move from a place to another, PPI will be ready to assist.

EARTH: Especially for families with children, and for elderly, who need to integrate in the new neighborhood.

USA, Washington (1790): Washington Monument (1848-1885, 169 m, 43 ha), on the National Mall, 700 m south of the White House.

Cooperation

SUN: People need to cooperate, in order to maintain peace.

EARTH: And PPI will be there to help, when needed.

Italy, Roma: From Ponte Palatino (1891), the remaining arch of the Pons Aemilius (178 BC, now called Ponte Rotto, left), Pons Fabricius (62 BC, right).

Prevention of accidents

SUN: Accidents always create stress and difficult situations.

EARTH: PPI will have useful information for prevention of accidents.

USA, New York (1624): on Broadway, close to Times Square, and to Times Square Tower (2004, 221 m, 47 floors).

Japan: In Shinjuku, Shinjuku Center Building (223 m, 54 fl, 1979, left), Mode Gakuen Cocoon Tower (204 m, 50 fl, 2008, center-left), Keio Plaza Hotel North Tower (180 m, 47 fl, 1971, center-right).

Commerce

SUN: Commerce is a stimulant of peace.

EARTH: Therefore will be promoted and encouraged by PPI.

France, Paris: Place de la Concorde (1772): the north fountain (1840, with figures of the rivers Rhone and Rhine), Hotel de Crillon (1758, left), Rue Royale, Église de la Madeleine and Marine Nationale (center).

Jobs

SUN: Good civilian jobs create a peaceful atmosphere.

EARTH: And PPI will be most interested to help.

Italy, Roma: Part of the Imperial Palaces (27 BC) on the Palatine Hill, north of the Circus Maximus (550 BC – 549 AD), the world largest stadium

Retirement

SUN: In retirement people are eager to have tranquility and peace.

EARTH: Very important for PPI to have in mind, and to help.

UK, Oxford: From Broad St, looking northwest to Trinity College (1555) buildings (right), and Balliol College (1263, center left).

Rural preparation for peace

SUN: How do you work in the rural area?

EARTH: Contacts with farmers, and others from the rural area, will be established by e-mails, video, phone, fax, letters and direct visits – it is an important factor in the preparation for peace.

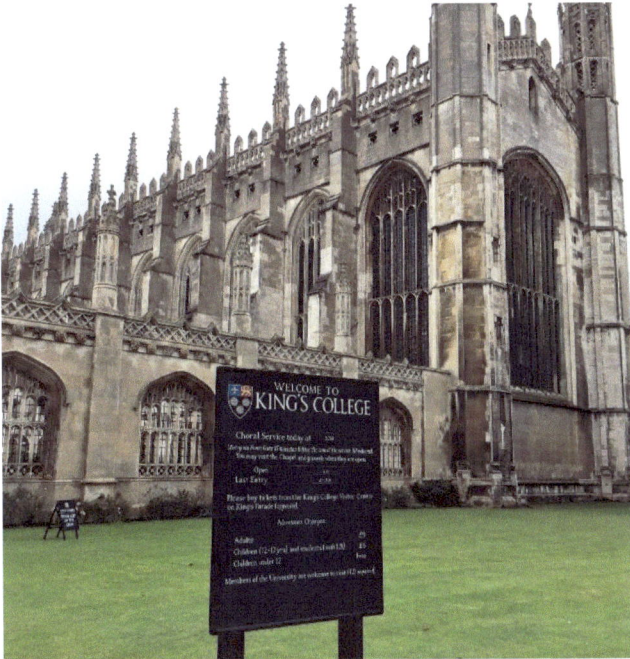

UK, Cambridge: From the entrance to King's College (1441), looking northwest to the Chapel (the south façade (center left), and the east façade (right))

Refugees from disasters

SUN: Flooding, hurricanes, earthquakes, volcanos, and other natural disasters create sometimes serious refugees' problems.

EARTH: And PPI will be there to help keep the peace.

Italy, Roma: The south-est side of the Templum Veneris et Romae (Temple of Venus and Rome) built by Emperor Hadrian in 135, 100 m x 145 m.

Peaceful relations at work

SUN: You know, at work appear stressful conflicts.

EARTH: Yes, and they must be properly managed in order to restore harmony, and PPI will be ready to assist, when needed.

UK, London: On Merton St, another building belonging to Merton College (1264)

Japan: In Shinjuku, the square in front of Tokyo Metropolitan Government Building (down), Shinjuku Sumitomo Bldg (210 m, 52 fl, 1974, center-left), Shinjuku Mitsui Building (224 m, 55 floors, 1974, right up).

Land disputes

SUN: Land disputes are the oldest and most frequent cause of serious conflicts.

EARTH: Indeed, and they require most attention – PPI will allocate resources to assist people to maintain peace.

SUN: Sometimes fences are needed.

EARTH: Good fences make good neighbors.

UK, Oxford: From Broad St, looking southeast to the north façade of Clarendon Building, the registration ceremony at the University of Oxford.

Water

SUN: Access to water is a burning issue in many places.

EARTH: Yes, and good solutions must be found – PPI will carefully address these problems, to keep peace.

SUN: The sewer also must be working well.

EARTH: Otherwise there is conflict, and we don't need this – PPI will always work for peace.

Italy, Roma: The south side of the Arch (315) of Constantine (272 – 337, Roman Emperor 306 - 337), from Via di San Gregorio.

Religious activity

SUN: Much care is needed for religious activities.

EARTH: Fortunately, many religious activities are very peaceful, and help preparing for peace. Those which are not so peaceful will need special attention, and PPI will help accordingly.

Italy, Rome, Vatican, Piazza San Pietro (1667, by Gian Lorenzo Bernini): Basilica di San Pietro (1506, center back), granite fountain by Carlo Maderno (1614, center, north side of piazza).

New York (1624): The north-east side of Times Square, with the 7th Avenue on the right and Broadway on the left, and with Morgan Stanley building (1989, 209 m, 42 floors), on the west side of Broadway (left). On the south-east side of Times Square there is the Conde Nast Building (1996-1999, 264 m, 48-story office tower), and on the west side there is Marriott Marquis building (1985, 175 m, 56 floors above ground, 2 floors below ground, 3 m floor to floor height).

Sport

SUN: Occasionally, sport events become violent.

EARTH: This needs to be addressed, and PPI will play a role in maintaining the peace.

Finland, Helsinki: a tall ship in the tourist harbor, in the south-east part of the city.

Tourism

SUN: Tourism is really important in the preparation for peace.

EARTH: PPI will actively support civilized tourism in all directions.

Italy, Roma: The south-west side of the Amphitheatrum Flavium (80 AD, Colosseum), built by Vespasian Flavius and his son Titus.

Beautification

SUN: Using peace related art and decorations for beautification is really pleasant.

EARTH: PPI will have plenty of ideas, and will help anytime.

USA, Washington, D.C. (1790): George Washington (1732-1799, first President 1789-1797) Monument (1848-1885, 169 m, 43 ha), on the National Mall, 700 m south of the White House, seen from the Constitution Avenue NW.

Japan: In Shinjuku, from the 45th fl., 202 m, of Tokyo Metropolitan. Gov Bldg: Shinjuku Park Tower (235 m, 52 fl, 1994, right).

Nobility

SUN: These days the royal families and their relatives are interested in peace.

EARTH: PPI will stay in touch with them to work together for peace.

Finland, Helsinki: The Railway Square, east of the railway station, with the Finnish National Theatre (1872 - 1902).

Medical personnel

SUN: How do you see the collaboration with the medical personnel?

EARTH: Very intense and friendly – PPI will always be hand in hand with the medical personnel, who work for peace day in day out. World Diabetes Day (November 14) helps raise awareness of diabetes, which is a growing epidemic. A new World Health Organization (WHO)-led study says majority of adolescents worldwide are not sufficiently physically active, putting their current and future health at risk. The first ever global trends for adolescent insufficient physical activity show that urgent action is needed to increase physical activity levels in girls and boys aged 11 to 17 years. Published by The Lancet Child & Adolescent Health

Italy, Roma: Temple of Saturn (42 BC, center-left up), Curia (283, center up), Nerva's Forum (97, down), Forum Caesaris (46 BC, center-right)

Veterans

SUN: Veterans and other military related people do need some extra attention.

EARTH: PPI will have a separate section for them, because they need explanations why it is better to switch to a civilian job.

SUN: Good civilian jobs should be found.

EARTH: This indeed requires extra work.

USA, Washington, DC (1790): the entrance to the Smithsonian Institution Building (1849-1855), on Jefferson Drive SW

Community living

SUN: Peaceful community living is a priority.

EARTH: PPI will certainly be involved in many communities, to explain the benefits of preparing for peace.

France, Paris: A new entrance on the south-east part of the Gare du Nord (1846), from Place Napoléon III (1808 – 1873, nephew of Napoleon I).

5 - Other tasks

Home visits

SUN: What about home visits?

EARTH: PPI will have extensive home visits, especially for people with medical problems and elderly, to create a peace-oriented atmosphere.

Italy, Roma: The Arch of Constantine (315, left) and Amphitheatrum Flavium (80 AD, Colosseum, right), from Via di San Gregorio

Police collaboration

SUN: Preparing for peace includes a strong collaboration with civilized and polite police.

EARTH: Yes, police must maintain order, stop aggressive people, take care of accidents, disasters, etc.

France, Paris: Grands Magasins du Printemps (1865, 1874, 1881, 1921) on Boulevard Haussmann (left) and Rue de Caumartin (right).

Japan: In Shinjuku, from the 45th fl., 202 m, of Tokyo Met. Gov Bldg South Tower: Shinjuku Mitsui Building (224 m, 55 floors, 1974, left), Shinjuku Center Building (223 m, 54 floors, 1979, center), Mode Gakuen Cocoon Tower (204 m, 50 floors, 2008, right up), Keio Plaza Hotel (180 m, 47 fl, 1971, right).

Arms elimination

SUN: It is understood that a sustainable peace can be achieved by eliminating all the arms.

EARTH: PPI will continuously work on this important problem.

France, Paris: Place de la Concorde (1772): The Egyptian obelisk (Ramses the Great, 1250 BC, 23 m), Marine Nationale (Navy, 1758, left).

UK, Oxford: From Merton St. looking south to the northern façade of the main entrance of Merton College (1264). Personalities associated with Merton College are British chemist Frederick Soddy (1877-1956, Nobel Prize in Chemistry (1921)), poet T. S. Elliot (1888 in St Louis, U. S. – 1965 in London, England, Nobel Prize in Literature (1948)), British philosopher John R. Lucas (born 1932), British mathematician Sir Andrew Wiles (born 1953, proved Fermat's (1607-1665) Last Theorem (1637) proved after 358 years).

World cooperation

SUN: Preparing for peace is a world effort.

EARTH: Therefore world cooperation is necessary.

Italy, Roma: Templum Sacrae Urbis (211) restored by Septimius Severus.

France, Paris: L'Église de la Sainte-Trinité (1861 – 1867, Roman Catholic church located in the 9th arrondissement of Paris, designed by Théodore Ballu, under the improvement and restructuring plan of Paris done by Baron Haussmann (1809 – 1891), chosen for this job by Emperor Napoleon III (1808–1873); bell tower 63 m high topped by a dome; recently had as organist the renowned composer Olivier Messiaen (1908-1992). It was the funeral place of Hector Berlioz (1803 – 1869) and Georges Bizet (1838 – 1875)).

Training

SUN: What about training?

EARTH: PPI will have a section dedicated to training employees and others for this preparation for peace.

UK, London: On Bow St, Royal Opera House at Covent Garden (1732, 1808, 1858, 1999, capacity 2,256). In 1734, Covent Garden presented its first ballet, Pygmalion.

USA, Bretton Woods: The Gold Room in the Mount Washington Resort (1902, elevation 500 m, by Joseph Stickney (1840 – 1903, coal business)), where the documents of the United Nations Monetary and Financial Conference (1 – 22 July 1944, 730 delegates from 44 Allied nations, at Bretton Woods (12 km west of Mount Washington (1917 m), 250 km north of Boston), established the International Monetary Fund and the World Bank. The Bretton Woods system worked for 27 years, until 1971) were signed. On the right - a table with the flags of the 44 Allied nations.

Young generation

SUN: Always pay attention to the young generation.

EARTH: They are the future, and PPI will permanently work with young people for peace.

UK, Oxford: Inside Weston Library, part of the Bodleian Libraries of the University of Oxford, Louis Pasteur (1822-1895) and Robert Koch (1843-1910), with milestones of discovery and innovation,

Qualified personnel

SUN: It is necessary to have qualified people.

EARTH: PPI will look for well qualified people in all fields, because peace is important for all.

Italy, Roma: Tabularium (78 BC, left), Severus' Arch (203, left), Curia (283, center-left), Caesar's Forum (46 BC, right), Altare della Patria (1925, right up).

Prevention first

SUN: How do you prevent violence and other bad events?

EARTH: Working closely with police and others, PPI will determine when a potential risk occurs, and rapidly intervene to calm down the situation.

France, Paris: La Seine River, from Pont d'Arcole, near l'Hôtel de Ville (1533), with Pont Notre Dame (center-right) and Conciergerie (center).

Japan: In Shinjuku, from the 45th fl., 202 m, of Tokyo Met. Gov Bldg North Tower): Shinjuku Sumitomo Bldg (210 m, 52 fl, 1974, center), Shinjuku Mitsui Building (224 m, 55 floors, 1974, right).

Education work

SUN: How do you approach education?

EARTH: PPI will be in contact with all schools, universities and other educational institutions, in order to implement a preparation for peace program at different levels of education.

UK, London: Inside the Covent Garden Market, with an opera soprano performing (center right down).

World library

SUN: You need a library for peace-related books, etc.

EARTH: PPI will work hard to have a world library, with facilities in many places in the world.

Italy, Roma: Templum Antonini et Faustina (141) built by Emperor Antoninus Pius (86 – 161, Emperor 138 – 161) for his wife Faustina.

Adult education for peace

SUN: Any adult education?

EARTH: Of course, peace is important for any age, therefore adult education for preparing for peace has a high priority for PPI.

UK, London: Inside (southeast corner) the British Museum (1753), an equestrian statue from the Roman Empire period (circa 39 BC).

France, Paris: La Tour Eiffel (1889, 324 m, 279 m third level observatory) seen from 2 km east in the south-west part of Place de la Concorde (1772, Louis XV), with the statue representing the city Bordeaux (center-left). Bordeaux is an inhabited historic port city in the south-west of France, 500 km south-west of Paris, the ninth largest city in France, in the Gironde department, on the Garonne River. The Bordeaux wines are famous for their excellent qualities.

Peace in fine arts and music

SUN: There is a long tradition of promoting peace through fine arts and music.

EARTH: And this tradition will be continued and extended.

UK, London: The southeast entrance of The British Museum (1753), exhibition "Sunken cities, Egypt's lost worlds, 19 May – 27 Nov 2016.

France, Paris: Musée du Louvre (1793): a statue representing art, in front of Pavillion Richelieu. in Cour Napoléon (1803). The Louvre is located on the right bank of La Seine, in the 1st arrondissement, and has about 35,000 museum objects, exhibited over an area of 60,600 m². With more than 8 million visitors each year, the Louvre is the world's most visited museum. The museum is housed in the Palais du Louvre, originally built as a fortress around 1190 under Philip II of France (1165 – 1223, king 1179 – 1223).

Peace and global media

SUN: Is global media helpful?

EARTH: In general yes, but PPI will work to have all global media support this preparation for peace.

Italia, Roma: Curia (283, left up), Forum Nervae (97, down), Forum Caesaris (46 BC, center-left up, Julius Caesar 100 BC – 44 BC).

UK, London, The Royal Albert Hall (1867-1871, 2004)– an Italian style concert hall on Kensington Gore, on the northern edge of South Kensington, capacity 5,272 seats, 41 m height, named after Prince Consort Albert (1819 (in Germany)-1861), husband (1840-1861) of Queen Victoria (1819-1901, Queen 1837-1901, had 9 children), Chancellor of the University of Cambridge from 1847. In July 1871, French organist and composer Camille Saint-Saëns (1835-1921) performed *Church Scene* from the Faust by Charles Gounod (1818-1893).

History of peace

SUN: Is there a history of peace?

EARTH: Most history books are about war and conflicts, but insistent work will be done to create a solid history of peace culture.

UK, London: From Merton St looking southeast to the east façade of the Merton College Chapel (1294, right), and the north façade of another building of Merton College (left, 1264), in the Front quad.

Japan: In Shinjuku, from the 45th fl., 202 m, of Tokyo Met. Gov Bldg North Tower): Shinjuku Sumitomo Bldg (210 m, 52 fl, 1974, left), Shinjuku Mitsui Building (224 m, 55 floors, 1974, 2nd left), Sompo Japan Building (193 m, 43 fl, 1976, center-left), Shinjuku Center Building (223 m, 54 floors, 1979, center), Mode Gakuen Cocoon Tower (204 m, 50 floors, 2008, center-right), Keio Plaza Hotel (180 m, 47 fl, 1971, right)..

Scholarships

SUN: Do you need peace scholarships?

EARTH: Yes, we'll have some, for the younger generation.

UK, London: From a bus on Oxford Street at South Molton St (right), looking east to Tissot store, and many other stores.

France, Paris: Musée du Louvre (1793): a statue representing science, in front of Pavillion Richelieu, in Cour Napoléon (1803). The Louvre is located on the right bank of La Seine, in the 1st arrondissement, and has about 35,000 museum objects, exhibited over an area of 60,600 m². With more than 8 millions of visitors each year, the Louvre is the world's most visited museum. The museum is housed in the Palais du Louvre, originally built as a fortress around 1190 under Philip II of France (1165 – 1223, king 1179 – 1223).

Science & technology for peace

SUN: Any idea?

EARTH: We'll have intense applications of mathematics, science and technology in the preparation for peace.

Italy, Roma: Forum Nervae (97, down), Forum Augusti (2 BC, with Temple of Mars Ultor, built with white marble of Carrara, center-right-up).

Cyberspace and peace

SUN: The cyberspace was invented for peaceful collaboration.

EARTH: Yes, and we will make sure that it will be used only for peaceful collaboration.

UK, Oxford: Oriel College (1326, in the back: the east range of First quadrangle, with ornate portico in the center)).

France, Paris: Avenue des Champs-Élysées (built by Louis XIV in 1670, 1910 m by 70 m); nicely decorated buildings (built around 1850), on the south side of the avenue, starting at the number 103, between Rue Galilée to the west and Rue de Bassano to the east.

Economic development and peace

SUN: How you see this issue?

EARTH: We'll certainly work hard to transform all the economy to be for peace purposes, and thus to have a very robust development for products people need, like good infrastructure everywhere, roads, bridges, water, sewer, electricity, gas, transportation, etc. The transport industry's improvement will be among the world government's highest priorities. The key objectives include upgrading the transit infrastructure, building major logistic hubs and international trade corridors, designing reliable and safe modes of transportation, and optimizing management solutions. It is important to integrate innovative technology more actively, and use the private-public partnership mechanisms more extensively.

I should add that the correct inflation rate in the U.S. on 18 November 2019 was 5%, compared to one year ago. The inflation includes CPI, weighted stock inflation, and weighted budget deficit inflation.

There are continued increases in the general level of prices of goods, services, stocks, as well as budget deficits.

The correct inflation rate in the world on 18 November 2019 was 6.2%, compared to one year ago. The inflation includes CPI, weighted stock inflation, and weighted budget deficit inflation.

There are continued increases in the general level of prices of goods, services, stocks, as well as budget deficits. Because of this the world economy will have difficulties.

UK, Oxford: On Merton Street an entrance to Corpus Christy College (1517, founder Richard Foxe, Bishop of Winchester, 12th oldest college in Oxford (1st University College (1249, 2nd Balliol College (1263), 3rd Merton College (1264)), 249 undergraduates, 94 postgraduates), situated between Merton College (founder Walter de Merton (1205-1277), Lord Chancellor to Henry III (1207-1272) and later to Edward I (1239-1307), and Catholic Bishop of Rochester (1274-1277); Merton College Library (1373) is the oldest functioning library in the world), and Oriel College (1326).

Japan, Shinjuku, one of the 23 special wards of Tokyo, with Shinjuku Mitsui Building (224 m, 55 floors, 1974, left), Shinjuku Center Building (223 m, 54 floors, 1979, center), Mode Gakuen Cocoon Tower (204 m, 50 floors, 2008, center-right).

Tokyo started around 1150 as a small fishing village named Edo (which means estuary). Edo was first fortified by the Edo clan, around 1180. In 1457 Edo Castle was built. In 1590 Tokugawa Ieyasu transformed Edo into his base and later, in 1603, the town became the center of his nationwide military government. Between 1603 and 1868 (Edo period), the city Edo developed into one of the biggest cities in the world, with a population of over one million by 1700. Its name was changed to Tokyo (east capital) when it became the imperial capital in 1868.

The population of the main city is over 9 million people; with the closest suburbs the total population exceeds 13 millions. The world's most populous metropolitan area is Tokyo, with circa 35 million people, and it also is the world's largest urban agglomeration economy, with a GDP of $1.479 trillion at purchasing power parity. The city is home for 51 of the Fortune Global 500 companies, the highest number for any city. The tallest structure in Tokyo is Tokyo Skytree (a lattice tower, 634 m, 2012).

Public works for peace

SUN: Usually the public works are peace-oriented.

EARTH: Yes, and we will extend this for all public works.

Italia, Roma: Templum Saturni (42 BC, right up), the Column of Phocas (608, center-right), Basilica Aemilia (Marcus Aemilius, 179 BC, down).

Risk analysis

SUN: Is it necessary?

EARTH: Yes, there is always some risk in all activities, and a mathematical risk analysis is useful.

Japan, A building with a modern amphitheater at Tokyo Denki University (TDU, founded in 1907) in the north-east of the Inzai (Chiba) campus, in Muzai-Gakuendai, 34 km north-east of Tokyo.

Artificial Intelligence (AI) and peace

SUN: Again, AI was created for peaceful applications.

EARTH: Indeed, and we will insist to remain only this way. AI technologies make it possible to get rid of the inertia and slowness of the bureaucratic machine, and to radically increase transparency and efficiency of administrative procedures. AI has capabilities to solve the problems of each person, and ultimately to change the quality of the entire system of public administration. AI can help to have comfortable and safe cities, accessible and high-quality healthcare and education, modern logistics and a reliable transportation system, exploration of space and the world ocean, sustainable and balanced development, the growing quality of life and new opportunities for people.

France, Paris (250 BC): l'Hôtel de Ville (City Hall since 1357, King Francis I started this building in 1533, finished 1628, 1873-1892.

France, Paris: Hotel Napoleon on Avenue de Friedland, 400 m east of l'Arc de Triomphe de l'Étoile, close to Rue Balzac and the statue of Honoré de Balzac (1799 – 1850). Napoleon Bonaparte (1769-1821, emperor of the French1804-1814, 1815, king of Italy 1805-1814), of Italian origin, played a significant role in the history of France and of the world. His legal reform, known as the Napoleonic Code, has influenced many civil law jurisdictions worldwide.

Peace research

SUN: Peace does not mean only no war.

EARTH: Exactly, peace also includes harmony, friendship and prosperity – research is needed to develop these areas.

UK, Oxford: On Oriel Street, looking southeast to the west façade of Oriel College (1326), Merton St, Corpus Christy College (1517, right).

Peaceful nuclear energy use

SUN: Nothing wrong with peaceful nuclear energy use.

EARTH: Of course, and, at the same time, the elimination of all nuclear arms is a very high priority.

Japan: A nice sculpture on the Inzai (Chiba) campus of Tokyo Denki University (TDU, founded in 1907) in Muzai-Gakuendai, 34 km north-east of Tokyo.

World resources for peace

SUN: It is important to have all the world resources used for peaceful purposes only.

EARTH: Absolutely, PPI will insist on this every day.

France, Paris: Cathédrale Notre Dame de Paris (1163 – 1345, 90 m, right), from l'Esplanade de la Liberation, in front of l'Hôtel de Ville (1533).

Broadcasting for peace

SUN: What about this?

EARTH: It would be very useful, and hopefully it will be achieved as soon as possible.

UK, London: From the northeast corner of Trafalgar Square looking west to the southeast façade of The National Gallery (1824, 2,300 paintings).

Space exploration

SUN: Space exploration was always peaceful.

EARTH: Yes, and it must remain this way – nobody wants to have nuclear bombs over their heads!

Japan: The front of a small laboratory on the Inzai (Chiba) campus of Tokyo Denki University (TDU, founded in 1907) in Muzai-Gakuendai, 34 km north-east of Tokyo.

Ten regions

SUN: What about these ten regions?

EARTH: They are important for a sustainable peace, freedom and prosperity, therefore the preparation for peace should include a preparation for these ten regions.

Let's remember the new 10 regions, called R0, R1,..., R9, which will be delimited (for easier administration) by meridians (or line of longitudes), with the assistance of the United Nations, each region having a pair of capitals (which will change every year), for example:

R0 between meridians 0 and 15^0 E, capitals: Bern and Libreville (Gabon)

R1: 15^0 E - 30^0 E, Warsaw (Poland) and Pretoria (South Africa)

R2: 30^0 E - 45^0 E, Moscow and Cairo

R3: 45^0 E - 75^0 E, Astana (Kazakhstan) and Karachi (Pakistan)

R4: 75^0 E - 85^0 E, New Delhi (India) and Tomsk (Russia)

R5: 85^0 E - 100^0 E, Kuala Lumpur (Malaysia) and Quanzhou (China)

R6: 100^0 E - 115^0 E, Jakarta (Indonesia) and Beijing

R7: 115^0 E - 180^0, Tokyo and Sydney (Australia)

R8: 180^0 - 70^0 W, Washington and Mexico City

R9: 70^0 W – 0, Halifax (Canada) and Brasilia

UK, Oxford: On St Aldate's St, 200 m north of Broad Walk, 80 m east of Pembroke College, Tom Tower (1682, bell (rung 101 times (every 12 seconds, it takes 20 minutes) at 9 PM every night) tower) over Tom Gate, the main entrance to the majestic Christ Church College (1546, 431 undergraduates, 250 postgraduates, the second wealthiest Oxford college (after St John's), produced 13 British prime ministers), leads into its grand Tom Quad (inside).

World government

SUN: Naturally, somebody has to administer the world for people's benefit and for peace.

EARTH: Yes, and there is a good book by our friend Michael M. Dediu: "Friendly, Helpful & Smart World Management - Moving from bureaucracy to responsive world management"

Japan: Inzai Post Office, 300 m north-est from the entrance to the Inzai (Chiba) campus of Tokyo Denki University (TDU, founded in 1907) in Muzai-Gakuendai, 34 km north-east of Tokyo.

World Constitution

SUN: Then a world constitution would be useful.

EARTH: Yes, and we have it in Michael M. Dediu's book "Our Future is Sustainable Peace and Prosperity – Moving from conflicts to harmony and peace"

The following are the main World Constitution subjects:
- rules
- small World Government, with 7 small departments
- elections - every 20 months for one term only, based on exceptional results, no propaganda
- advisors' levels - minimum age 25 years, First Adviser for one month, by rotation
- assistants
- administrators
- Honorific Word Observer
- medical assistance, Specialized Medical Institutions for disorderly behavior
- people assistance services
- some police with small arms
- total disarmament
- no conflicts
- no war
- no military forces
- no arms
- no abuses
- freedom and responsibility
- people can assemble peacefully only
- census: **A census will take place every 5 years – starting, let's say on October 1st, 2023 - and all the people will receive a special credit card (SCC), with their photo and other personal data.**
- special credit card **with photo and other personal data. The special credit card (SCC) will be used to buy everything, to identify for voting, for census, for travel, for medical assistance, etc.**

- World Central Bank: **The SCC will be issued by the World Central Bank, which will include all current central banks – starting, let's say on May 1st, 2023.**

    - new world currency
    - budgets with surplus
    - tax: 15% of income
    - no borrowing
    - 40 hours/week, compensation
    - savings accounts for old age
    - International standards
    - Intellectual Property
    - World Post Offices
    - free commerce and collaboration
    - common sense
    - prevention of bad events first - if bad, then pay all expense and reimburse
    - language and alphabet

France, Paris: Place de la Concorde: the north side of the Egyptian obelisk (circa 1250 BC), with hieroglyphics about the pharaoh Ramses the Great (1303 BC – 1213 BC (90 years), reign 1279 BC – 1213 BC (66 years)). The obelisk is from Luxor, rises 23 m, weights 250 t and it was placed here by the King Louis Philippe I (1773 – 1850, reign 1830 – 1848) in 1836, On the pedestal are drawn diagrams showing the techniques used for transportation. The original cap was stolen in Luxor around 550 BC, and the French Government added a gold-leafed pyramid cap in 1998.

Good Managers

SUN: Great! Do you happen to also have some examples of good managers?

EARTH: But of course!

- Jeff Bezos, $131 B, U.S., started Amazon in his garage in 1994, and now he is the richest man in the world. He allocates $1 billion a year to space travel.

- Bill Gates, $96.5 B, U.S., Microsoft co-founder.

- Warren Buffett, $82.5, U.S., Berkshire Hathaway CEO.

- Bernard Arnault, $76 B, French billionaire who owns LVMH, parent company to brands such as Louis Vuitton and Sephora. He is the richest man in Europe.

- Amancio Ortega, 83, $69.7 B, Spain, the cofounder of Inditex, the conglomerate which owns clothing giant Zara; he is the richest retailer in the world.

- Carlos Slim Helú, $64, Mexico, is the head of telecom company América Móvil, making him the richest man in Latin America. He also has investments in construction, real estate and mining.

- Larry Ellison, $62.5, U. S., Oracle cofounder.

- Larry Page, $50.8 B, U.S. is the Google cofounder.

- Charles Koch, $50.5, U.S. has headed up Koch Industries since 1967.

- Mukesh Ambani, $50 B, India, inherited Reliance Industries from his father, Dhirubhai Ambani. The oil and gas company now has revenues of $90 B, meaning Ambani is the richest man in Asia.

France, Paris: The main entrance of the old building of Gare du Nord (1846, 1865). The sculptures represent the principal cities served by this station. The statue in the center up, near the flag, represents Paris, the other eight (only four visible left up) of the nine most majestic statues, topping the building along the cornice line, illustrate destinations outside France. Fourteen more modest statues, representing northern French cities, are lower on the façade.

- Sergey Brin, $49.8 B, U.S., the cofounder of Google, heads up Google's parent company Alphabet, and also ran Google X.

- Jim Walton, $44.6 B, U. S., the youngest son of Walmart founder Sam Walton

- Rob Walton, $44.3 B, U. S., the eldest son of Walmart founder Sam Walton.

- Steve Ballmer, $41.2, U.S., is a businessman and investor who became a billionaire because of the stock he received as CEO of Microsoft from 2000 to 2014.

- Ma Huateng, $38.8 B, co-founded internet company Tencent in 1998, and is China's richest man.

- Jack Ma, $37.3 B, China, cofounder of the hugely successful e-commerce giant Alibaba Group.

- Phil Knight, 81, $36.6 B, U.S., owes much of his wealth to sportswear giant Nike, which he founded in 1964.

- Hui Ka Yan, $36.2, China, is chairman of real estate development empire the Evergrande Group.

- Sheldon Adelson, $35.1 B, U. S., is the CEO of casino chain Las Vegas Sands

- Michael Dell, $34.3 B, is the CEO of Dell Technologies, although most of his wealth comes from his investments in commercial property.

- David Thomson, $32.5 B, is the richest man in Canada. His wealth comes from the publishing empire built by his grandfather Roy, which includes Thomson Reuters.

In Shinjuku, from the 45th fl., 202 m, of Tokyo Metropolitan. Gov Bldg North Tower: part of South Tower of Tokyo Metropolitan. Gov Bldg (243 m, 48 floors, 1991, left), Shinjuku Park Tower (235 m, 52 fl, 1994, center-left), Tokyo Opera City Tower (234 m, 54 fl, 1996, center-right), Shinjuku Central Park (down).

- Li Ka-shing, $31.7, China, one of the most successful entrepreneurs in Asia. Li retired in 2018, but still acts as senior adviser to CK Hutchison Holdings and CK Asset Holdings, two conglomerates with multiple investments.

- Lee Shau-kee, 91, $30.1, Hong Kong, came from humble beginnings. He founded Henderson Land Development in 1976, and also co-owns property development firm Sun Hung Kai.

- François Pinault, $29.7 B, France, built and chairs the Kering Group. Founded in 1963, it began life as a building supplies company, and now owns fashion houses including Gucci and Alexander McQueen.

- Joseph Safra, 81, $24.7, Brazil, born in Aleppo, Syria, is the world's richest banker.

- Leonid Mikhelson, $24 B, Russia, built and chairs natural gas company Novatek. He is the richest man in Russia.

- John Mars, $23.9 B, U.K., inherited his fortune from the family's confectionery business when his father died in 1999. Mars Inc. was founded in 1911 by John's grandfather, Frank.

- Jorge Paulo Lemann, $22.8, Brazil, made his fortune through investment banking, and then as a shareholder of brewing giant Anheuser-Busch InBev. He is a co-founder of investment group 3G Capital, which joined forces with Warren Buffett's Berkshire Hathaway in 2013 in order to acquire the H. J. Heinz Co. for $28 B.

- Dieter Schwarz, $22.6 B, Germany, from his father Josef, who founded Schwarz Gruppe, which owns supermarket chain Lidl.

- Wang Jianlin, $22.6 B, China, is chairman of Dalian Wanda Group, China's largest real estate developer, which has a massive commercial property portfolio, including 260 plazas across China. In 2017 he sold his China hotel and tourism empire for $9 B.

UK, Cambridge: From Trinity Lane looking south to the west part of the northern façade and entrance of King's College Chapel (1446, center back, the College was founded in 1441, and the Old Schools was part of King's College), the east gate of Clare College (1326, as University Hall, making it the second-oldest college of the University, after Peterhouse (1284)) and its Chapel (1763, center right), and the Old Schools (1441, University Offices, left).

- Azim Premji, $22.6, India, dropped out of Stanford University in 1966 in order to head up the family business after the death of his father. After Premji shifted the cooking oil enterprise into the software industry, the company, renamed Wipro, became extremely lucrative.

- Giovanni Ferrero, $22.4 B, Italy, heads up the family's Ferrero confectionery empire. He acquired U.K. chocolatier Thorntons for $140 millions in 2015, the Ferrara Candy Co. for $1.3 B in 2017 and Nestle's American confectionery business for $2.8 B in 2018. In April it was announced that the Ferrero Group would also purchase multiple well-known brands from Kellogg for $1.3 B.

- Tadashi Yanai, $22.2 B, the richest man in Japan, founded and runs the Fast Retailing fashion group, which owns Uniqlo. The billionaire is aiming to overtake Inditex, and become the world's biggest retailer

Japan: 250 m north-est of the main entrance to the Inzai (Chiba) campus of Tokyo Denki University, with the supercenter Trial, a blue sign shows that the city Kikari is ahead (1 km north), Kamagaya is to the left (west) on route 464 (9 km), and Narita, with a big international airport, is to the right (east) on route 464 (20 km).

- Vagit Alekperov, 69, $22 B, the president of the leading Russian oil company LUKOIL.

- Masayoshi Son, $21.6 B, Japanese founder and CEO of investment firm SoftBank. The company's investment arm, the Vision Fund, is the biggest tech fund in history, and has made investments in Uber, WeWork, Yahoo Japan, Slack and Brightstar. The Japanese billionaire

- James Simons, retired, $21.5 B, U.S., found Renaissance Technologies in 1982. The hedge fund currently manages more than $110 B.

- Vladimir Lisin, $21.3 B, Russian chairman of metals manufacturer NLMK

France, Paris: Pavillions Richelieu (left) and Sully (right) on the north and east parts of Musée du Louvre, after Place du Carrousel and Pyramid.

Conclusions

SUN: Now, pour la bon bouche, what you have to say?

EARTH: - Let's start with children - if all over 2 billions of children in the world will get a solid peace-oriented education (see Dediu's book at number 90 in bibliography: Our Future Depends on Good World Educations – Moving from frail education to solid education), our future will be in good hands!

SUN: What is the purpose of education?

EARTH: Simply, to give a solid peace-oriented foundation for a good, free, peaceful and prosperous life.

SUN: Now tell me, what is the purpose for all over 7.7 billions of people on you?

EARTH: Good question: it is to be healthy, to live in peace, freedom and harmony, to be prosperous, and to prepare to expand to the Moon, asteroids, Mars, and other places in the Universe, which can support life.

SUN: I see, you want them to go to my other planets and asteroids, and even out of my Solar system! That's great! And what ideas do you have for their future?

EARTH: First of all, they must have a good World Government, as described in Dediu's book "Friendly, Helpful & Smart World Management - Moving from bureaucracy to responsive world management". Then they will do the following:
- Reserve time for happiness
- Use robots and automated processes, work less, and spend more time with their families
- The weekend will be like a small vacation
- Prevent burnout
- Make civilized harmony everywhere an important issue
- Eliminate stress

- Help friends and colleagues
- Keep everybody relaxed, calm, friendly, patient, and happy.

SUN: Excellent! That's the way to go, and I wish you all good health and great success!

EARTH: Thank you, Sun, and please continue to send us your energy, light, and so many other good things, without which we cannot live.

SUN: I cannot refuse you; you'll have them all, and enjoy the Sun!

Japan: A blooming tree (left) in the mid of November 2008, near an artesian fountain in the central park from the Inzai (Chiba) campus of Tokyo Denki University, at sunset.

Bibliography

"The Histories" by Polybius
"Discours de la Méthode" by René Descartes
"Meditationes de prima philosophia" by René Descartes
"Philosophiae Naturalis Principia Mathematica" by Isaac Newton
Chinese encyclopedia Gujin Tushu Jicheng (Imperial Enciclopaedia)
"Encyclopédie" by Jean-Baptiste le Rond d'Alembert and Denis Diderot
"Encyclopaedia Britannica" by over 4,400 contributors
"Encyclopedia Americana" by Francis Lieber
"Grand Larousse encyclopédique en 24 volumes" by Albert Ducrocq
Nobel Prize Organization
"The Cambridge History of Medicine", edited by Roy Porter
"Great Russian Encyclopedia" by Yury Osipov
"Encyclopedia of China"
"Enciclopedia Italiana di Scienze, Lettere ed Arti" (35 volume), by Giovanni Treccani
Concise Oxford Dictionary of Opera
"Allgemeine Encyclopädie der Wissenschaften und Künste" by Johann Samuel Ersch und Johann Gottfried Gruber
Grove Dictionary of Music and Musicians
"Gran Enciclopedia de España"
Other sources include: UPI, CNBC, AP, Nasdaq, Reuters, EDGAR, AFP, Recode, Europa Press, Bloomberg News, Fox News, USA, Deutsche Presse-Agentur, MSNBC, BBC, Australian Associated Press, Agência Brasil, The Canadian Press (La Presse Canadienne), Middle East News Agency, Baltic News Service, Suomen Tietotoimisto, Athens-Macedonian News Agency, Asian News International, Inter Press Service, Kyodo News, Notimex, Algemeen Nederlands Persbureau, AGERPRES, Newsis, Tidningarnas Telegrambyrå, Swiss Telegraphic Agency, Central News Agency, ANKA news agency, Agenzia Fides

The upper part of the western façade of Cathédrale Notre Dame de Paris (1163 – 1345, 90 m), on the south-eastern part of the Île de la Cité, which is considered the center of Paris, in the fourth arrondissement. The organ has 7,374 pipes, with about 900 classified as historical. It has 110 real stops, five 56-key manuals and a 32-key pedalboard; it is now fully computerized. The Towers at Notre-Dame contain five church bells. The great bourdon bell, Emmanuel, from 1681, 13 t, is located in the South Tower (right).

Michael M. Dediu is also the author of these books (which can be found on Amazon.com):

1. Aphorisms and quotations – with examples and explanations
2. Axioms, aphorisms and quotations – with examples and explanations
3. 100 Great Personalities and their Quotations
4. Professor Petre P. Teodorescu – A Great Mathematician and Engineer
5. Professor Ioan Goia – A Dedicated Engineering Professor
6. Venice (Venezia) – a new perspective. A short presentation with photographs
7. La Serenissima (Venice) - a new photographic perspective. A short presentation with many photos
8. Grand Canal – Venice. A new photographic viewpoint. A short presentation with many photos
9. Piazza San Marco – Venice. A different photographic view. A short presentation with many photos
10. Roma (Rome) - La Città Eterna. A new photographic view. A short presentation with many photos
11. Why is Rome so Fascinating? A short presentation with many photos
12. Rome, Boston and Helsinki. A short photographic presentation
13. Rome and Tokyo – two captivating cities. A short photographic presentation
14. Beautiful Places on Earth – A new photographic presentation
15. From Niagara Falls to Mount Fuji via Rome - A novel photographic presentation
16. From the USA and Canada to Italy and Japan - A fresh photographic presentation
17. Paris – Why So Many Call This City Mon Amour - A lovely photographic presentation
18. The City of Light – Paris (La Ville-Lumière) - A kaleidoscopic photographic presentation
19. Paris (Lutetia Parisiorum) – the romance capital of the world - A kaleidoscopic photographic view
20. Paris and Tokyo – a joyful photographic presentation. With a preamble about the Universe

France, Paris: Tour Eiffel (1889, 324 m, 279 m 3rd level, looking north-west): Tour Eiffel shadow (center-right down), Pont d'Iéna over Seine (center down), Av. de New York (on the north side of Seine), Jardin du Trocadéro (center-down), Chaillot Palace (middle), Av. du Président Wilson (green, horizontal, middle), Allée. Maria Callas (center to left up), Bois de Boulogne (green up), tall buildings in Courbevoie near Seine (up center, 4.5 km away).

21. From USA to Japan via Canada – A cheerful photographic documentary

22. 200 Wonderful Places, In The Last 50 Years – A personal photographic documentary

23. Must see places in USA and Japan - A kaleidoscopic photographic documentary

24. Grandeurs of the World - A kaleidoscopic photographic documentary

25. Corneliu Leu – writer on the same wavelength as Mark Twain. An American viewpoint

26. From Berkeley to Pompeii via Rome – A kaleidoscopic photographic documentary

27. From America to Europe via Japan - A kaleidoscopic photographic documentary

28. Discover America and Japan - A photographic documentary

29. J. R. Lucas – philosopher on a creative parallel with Plato, An American viewpoint

30. From America to Switzerland via France - A photographic documentary

31. From Bretton Woods to New York via Cape Cod - A photographic documentary

32. Splendid Places on the Atlantic Coast of the U. S. A. - A photographic documentary

33. Fourteen nice Cities on three Continents - A photographic documentary

34. 17 Picturesque Cities on the World Map - A photographic documentary

35. Unforgettable Places from Four Continents including Trump buildings - A photographic documentary

36. Dediu Newsletter, Volume 1, Number 1, 6 December 2016 – Monthly news, review, comments and suggestions for a better and wiser world

37. Dediu Newsletter, Volume 1, Number 2, 6 January 2017 (available at www.derc.com).

38. Dediu Newsletter, Volume 1, Number 3, 6 February 2017 (available at www.derc.com).

39. London and Greenwich, A photographic documentary

UK, London: On Broad Ct looking northeast, off Bow Street to the northeast, 50 m north of the Royal Opera House at Covent Garden (1732, 1808, 1858, 1999, capacity 2,256; in 1734, Covent Garden presented its first ballet, Pygmalion), the bronze statue Young Dancer, by the Italian-born (in Mestre, near Venice, in 1921) British sculptor Enzo Plazzotta (1921-1981 (age 60)). To the right up, five red telephone boxes, at 5 Broad Ct, a tourist attraction.

40. Dediu Newsletter, Volume 1, Number 4, 6 March 2017 (available also at www.derc.com).

41. Dediu Newsletter, Volume 1, Number 5, 6 April 2017 (available also at www.derc.com).

42. Dediu Newsletter, Volume 1, Number 6, 6 May 2017 (available also at www.derc.com).

43. Dediu Newsletter, Volume 1, Number 7, 6 June 2017 (available also at www.derc.com).

44. London, Oxford and Cambridge, A photographic documentary

45. Dediu Newsletter, Volume 1, Number 8, 6 July 2017 (available also at www.derc.com).

46. Dediu Newsletter, Volume 1, Number 9, 6 August 2017 (available also at www.derc.com).

47. Dediu Newsletter, Volume 1, Number 10, 6 September 2017 (available also at www.derc.com).

48. Three Great Professors: President Woodrow Wilson, Historian Germán Arciniegas, Mathematician Gheorghe Vrănceanu, A chronological and photographic documentary

49. Dediu Newsletter, Volume 1, Number 11, 6 October 2017 (available also at www.derc.com).

50 Dediu Newsletter, Volume 1, Number 12, 6 November 2017 (available also at www.derc.com).

51 Dediu Newsletter, Volume 2, Number 1 (13), 6 December 2017 (available also at www.derc.com).

52 Two Great Leaders: Augustus and George Washington, A chronological and photographic documentary

53. Dediu Newsletter, Volume 2, Number 2 (14), 6 January 2018 (available also at www.derc.com).

54. Newton, Benjamin Franklin, and Gauss, A chronological and photographic documentary

55. Dediu Newsletter, Volume 2, Number 3 (15), 6 February 2018 (available also at www.derc.com).

56. 2017: World Top Events, But Many Little Known, A chronological and photographic documentary

57. Dediu Newsletter, Volume 2, Number 4 (16), 6 March 2018 (available also at www.derc.com).

58. Vergilius, Horatius, Ovidius, and Shakespeare, A chronological and photographic documentary.

UK, London: From Charing Cross Rd, looking southeast to the northwest part of the front part of the English Anglican church St Martin in the Fields (1724, at the northeast corner of Trafalgar Square in the City of Westminster, spire height 59 m, 12 bells, tenor bell weight 1,486 kg, excavations under found a grave from about 410 AD (Roman era), in 1222 there was a church here, in 1542 Henry VIII rebuilt the church, in 1606 James I enlarged the church). It is famous for its regular lunchtime and evening concerts; Academy of St Martin-in-the-Fields performs here, and many other ensembles.

59. Dediu Newsletter, Volume 2, Number 5 (17), 6 April 2018 (available also at www.derc.com).

60. Dediu Newsletter, Volume 2, Number 6 (18), 6 May 2018 (available also at www.derc.com).

61. Vivaldi, Bach, Mozart, and Verdi, A chronological and photographic documentary

62. Dediu Newsletter, Volume 2, Number 7 (19), 6 June 2018 (available also at www.derc.com).

63. Dediu Newsletter, Volume 2, Number 8 (20), 6 July 2018 (available also at www.derc.com).

64. Dediu Newsletter, Volume 2, Number 9 (21), 6 August 2018 (available also at www.derc.com).

65. World History, a new perspective - A chronological and photographic documentary.

66. World Humor History with over 100 Jokes, a new perspective - A chronological and photographic documentary

67. Dediu Newsletter, Vol 2, N 10 (22), 6 September 2018

68. Dediu Newsletter, Vol 2, N 11 (23), 6 October 2018

69. Da Vinci, Michelangelo, Rembrandt, Rodin - A chronological and photographic documentary

70. Dediu Newsletter, Vol 2, N 12 (24), 6 November 2018

71. Dediu Newsletter, Vol 3, N 1 (25), 6 December 2018

72. From Euclid to Edison - revelries in the last 75 years - A chronological and photographic documentary

73. Dediu Newsletter, Vol 3, N 2 (26), 6 January 2019

74. Socrates to Churchill - Aphorisms celebrated after 1960 - A chronological and photographic documentary

75. Dediu Newsletter Vol 3, Number 3 (27), 6 February 2019

76. Hippocrates to Fleming: Medicine History celebrated after 1943 - A chronological and photographic documentary

77. Dediu Newsletter, Volume 3, Number 4 (28), 6 March 2019

78. Dediu Newsletter, Volume 3, Number 5 (29), 6 April 2019

79. Archimedes to Ford: Invention History celebrated after 1943 - A chronological and photographic documentary

80. Dediu Newsletter, Volume 3, Number 6 (30), 6 May 2019

81. Sutherland to Pavarotti: Great Singers History - A chronological and photographic documentary

82. Dediu Newsletter, Volume 3, Number 7 (31), 6 June 2019

83. Dediu Newsletter, Volume 3, Number 8 (32), 6 July 2019

UK, Cambridge: From Trinity Ln, looking west through the entrance of Trinity Hall, (1350, by William Baterman (c 1298-1355, Bishop of Norwich between 1344 and 1355), a constituent college (the 5th oldest) of the University of Cambridge), to the Front Court and the entrance to the west building of the Front Court. To the northeast of Trinity Hall there is the separate Trinity College (1546, founder Henry VIII (1491-1547, reign 1509-1547), motto: Virtus Vera Nobilitas).

84. Augustus to Rockefeller: History of the Wealthiest People - A chronological and photographic documentary
85. Dediu Newsletter, Volume 3, Number 9 (33), 6 August 2019
86 – Pythagoras to Fermi: History of Science - A chronological and photographic documentary
87. Dediu Newsletter, Volume 3, Number 10 (34), 6 September 2019
88. Our Future is Sustainable Peace and Prosperity – Moving from conflicts to harmony and peace
89 - Dediu Newsletter, Volume 3, Number 11 (35), 6 October 2019 – World Monthly Report with News
90 – Our Future Depends on Good World Educations – Moving from frail education to solid education
91 - Dediu Newsletter, Volume 3, Number 12 (36), 6 November 2019 – World Monthly Report with News
92 – Friendly, Helpful & Smart World Management - Moving from bureaucracy to responsive world management

Japan: Wind turbine working on the north-west part of the Inzai (Chiba) campus of Tokyo Denki University, 34 km north-east of Tokyo.

Michael M. Dediu is the editor of these books (also on Amazon.com):

1. Sophia Dediu: The life and its torrents – Ana. In Europe around 1920
2. Proceedings of the 4th International Conference "Advanced Composite Materials Engineering" COMAT 2012
3. Adolf Shvedchikov: I am an eternal child of spring – poems in English, Italian, French, German, Spanish and Russian
4. Adolf Shvedchikov: Life's Enigma – poems in English, Italian and Russian
5. Adolf Shvedchikov: Everyone wants to be HAPPY – poems in English, Spanish and Russian
6. Adolf Shvedchikov: My Life, My Love – poems in English, Italian and Russian
7. Adolf Shvedchikov: I am the gardener of love – poems in English and Russian
8. Adolf Shvedchikov: Amaretta di Saronno – poems in English and Russian
9. Adolf Shvedchikov: A Russian Rediscovers America
10. Adolf Shvedchikov: Parade of Life - poems in English and Russian
11. Adolf Shvedchikov: Overcoming Sorrow - poems in English and Russian
12. Sophia Dediu: Sophia meets Japan
13. Corneliu Leu: Roosevelt, Churchill, Stalin and Hitler: Their surprising role in Eastern Europe in 1944
14. Proceedings of the 5th International Conference "Computational Mechanics and Virtual Engineering" COMEC 2013
15. Georgeta Simion – Potanga: Beyond Imagination: A Thought-provoking novel inspired from mid-20th century events
16. Ana Dediu: The poetry of my life in Europe and The USA
17. Ana Dediu: The Four Graces
18. Proceedings of the 5th International Conference "Advanced Composite Materials Engineering" COMAT 2014
19. Sophia Dediu: Chocolate Cook Book: Is there such a thing as too much chocolate?

UK, Cambridge: From Trinity Ln, looking west to the entrance of Trinity Hall (1350, a constituent college (the 5th oldest) of the University of Cambridge (1209, royal charter by King Henry III (1207-1272) in 1231, motto: Hinc lucem et pocula sacra (From here, light and sacred draughts), ranked the world's fourth best university, and the first in the UK, Sir Isaac Newton (1642-1727) was a student here, Charles Babbage (1791-1871, mathematician and father of the computer) student).

20. Sorin Vlase: Mechanical Identifiability in Automotive Engineering

21. Gabriel Dima: The Evolution of the Aerostructures – Concept and Technologies

22. Proceedings of the 6th International Conference "Computational Mechanics and Virtual Engineering" COMEC 2015

23. Sophia Dediu: Cook Book 1 A-B-C Common sense cooking

24. Sophia Dediu: Dim Sum Spring Festival

25. Ana Dediu and Sophia Dediu: Europe in 1985: A chronological and photographic documentary

26 Stefan Staretu: Europe: Serbian Despotate of Srem and the Romanian area. Between the 14th and the 16th Centuries

Japan: Photographs and computer presentations at the High Energy Accelerator Research Organization (KEK, 1997) in Tsukuba Science City (1962), in Ibaraki, 60 km north-east of Tokyo.

www.ingramcontent.com/pod-product-compliance
Lightning Source LLC
Chambersburg PA
CBHW041309210326
41599CB00003B/38